Instant VMware vCloud Starter

A practical, hands-on guide to get started with VMware vCloud

Daniel Langenhan

PUBLISHING

BIRMINGHAM - MUMBAI

Instant VMware vCloud Starter

First published: February 2013

Production Reference: 1180213

Published by Packt Publishing Ltd.
Livery Place
35 Livery Street
Birmingham B3 2PB, UK.
ISBN 978-1-84968-996-0

www.packtpub.com

Credits

Author

Daniel Langenhan

Reviewers

Andrew Crane

David Dean

Acquisition Editor

Rukhsana Khambatta

Commissioning Editor

Maria D'souza

Technical Editor

Chirag Jani

Copy Editor

Brandt D'Mello

Project Coordinator

Joel Goveya

Proofreader

Aaron Nash

Graphics

Aditi Gajjar

Production Coordinator

Melwyn D'sa

Cover Work

Melwyn D'sa

Cover Image

Sheetal Aute

About the Author

Daniel Langenhan is a client-focused virtualization expert with more than 18 years' experience in the international industry.

His skills span the breadth of virtualization, ranging from architecture, design, and implementation for large, multitier enterprise client systems, to delivering captivating education and training sessions in security technologies and practices to diverse audiences.

In addition, he possesses extensive knowledge of and experience in process management, enterprise-level storage, and Linux and Solaris operating systems.

Utilizing his extensive knowledge, experience, and skills, he has a proven track record of successfully integrating the virtualization process into different business areas, while minimizing the cost and maximizing the reliability and effectiveness of the solution for his clients.

He has gained experience with major Australian and international vendors and clients. Daniel's consulting company is well established with strong industry ties in many verticals, such as finance, telecommunications, and print. His consulting business also provides services to VMware International.

I would like to thank my wife Renata for her tireless support in all things.

About the Reviewers

Andrew Crane has over 25 years' experience in the IT industry in the field of IT architecture. His experience with large enterprise customer environments brings knowledge of an ever-changing industry, which is now firmly focused on private and public cloud platforms. For the design and deployment of vCloud solutions to align with business drivers is Andrew's major consultancy focus.

David Dean is a Senior Technology Specialist with expertise in networks, virtualization, automation, and operating systems at Australia's largest and most innovative companies. His interests lie in using automation and new technologies to deliver organizational value and create holistic lifecycles for complex systems. He has experience in raising large organizations from low levels of configuration management to full service delivery automation, including provisioning, application delivery, deployment, and eventual decommissioning. His recent work includes design and architecture on internal clouds for some of Australia's largest companies.

I'd like to thank my wife Josie for her support through the reviewing process.

www.packtpub.com

Support files, eBooks, discount offers and more

You might want to visit www.packtpub.com for support files and downloads related to your book.

Did you know that Packt offers eBook versions of every book published, with PDF and ePub files available? You can upgrade to the eBook version at www.packtpub.com and as a print book customer, you are entitled to a discount on the eBook copy. Get in touch with us at service@packtpub.com for more details.

At www.packtpub.com, you can also read a collection of free technical articles, sign up for a range of free newsletters and receive exclusive discounts and offers on Packt books and eBooks.

packtlib.packtpub.com

Do you need instant solutions to your IT questions? PacktLib is Packt's online digital book library. Here, you can access, read and search across Packt's entire library of books.

Why Subscribe?

✦ Fully searchable across every book published by Packt

✦ Copy and paste, print and bookmark content

✦ On demand and accessible via web browser

Free Access for Packt account holders

If you have an account with Packt at www.packtpub.com, you can use this to access PacktLib today and view nine entirely free books. Simply use your login credentials for immediate access.

Table of Contents

Instant VMware vCloud Starter

Welcome to *VMware vCloud Starter*. This book has been specially created to provide you with all the information that you need to get started with VMware vCloud. You will learn about the basics of installing and operating a Private Cloud environment using the VMware vCloud Suite 5.1 products.

This book contains the following sections:

So, what is a VMware vCloud? will tell you what a cloud is. Then it will discuss what a vCloud is, what it can do, and why it's such a hot topic.

Installation will teach you how to install a simple private cloud with ease and using minimal technology.

Quick start – creating your first VM will show you how to perform the core tasks with vCloud Director, such as provisioning a vApp.

Top 2 features you need to know about will teach you how to use the most powerful features of vCloud Director 5.1. By the end of this section, you will be able to create templates and provision VMs with isolated networks.

People and places you should get to know will list forums, websites, communities, and a list of useful documentation and white papers that will deepen your knowledge and understanding of the software.

So, what is VMware vCloud?

In this section we will discuss what a vCloud is, what it can do, and why it is such a hot topic.

What is a cloud?

When we start talking about the cloud, most people have various ideas about what it actually is and what it involves. There are many clouds out there, including the iCloud, the Amazon Cloud, the VMware Cloud, and so on. First, let's start with understanding what a cloud is by reading the following simplified example.

If you wanted a sandwich, in the traditional model, you would have had to go to the bakery to get some bread, to the butcher's to get some meat, and let's not forget about the cheese. This would be the old model where, first, you need to get all the hardware parts (disk, CPU, and so on) before assembling them and then finally be able to build your application. The next step in technology was virtualization, which is like a supermarket, where you can get everything in one place. Things are easier, but you still need to make the sandwich (install the operating system). In that sense, the cloud is basically like a sandwich shop; you tell the person behind the counter what you want and they deliver the finished product.

An industry-recognized definition of the cloud by the **National Institute of Standards and Technology (NIST)** is as follows:

> *Cloud computing is a model for enabling ubiquitous, convenient, and on-demand network access to a shared pool of configurable computing resources (for example, networks, servers, storage, applications, and services) that can rapidly be provisioned and released with minimal management effort or service provider interaction.*

What that means is:

+ The cloud is an interface that presents you with choices. It lets you create, interact with, and destroy your VMs and handles the user authentication. In our sandwich shop example, it would be the person serving you the sandwich.

+ A cloud abstracts resources. What this means is that you, as an end user, don't need to worry about the details of the storage, for example. You just choose the reliability, speed, and capacity that is needed. The cloud will automatically provide the right storage for you. The same is true for CPU, memory, and even the OS. In our sandwich example, it's the ingredients that are prepared and you can choose from the menu.

+ The cloud delivers services. This is the part that most people struggle with. A service is basically the end product (the sandwich we have been talking about in our example). Cloud services are defined in three different versions:

  ○ **Platform as a Service (PaaS)** provides fully provisioned VMs with an installed and configured operating system. In our example, it is a basic sandwich, where you still need to add your condiments.

- **Software as a Service (SaaS)** provides the end user with a fully installed and configured application, such as a database or a web server. In our example, it would be a ham sandwich where you don't mind the type of bread. Let's say you need an Apache web server but it doesn't matter if it's on Windows or Linux.

- **Infrastructure as a Service (IaaS)** provides other infrastructures such as firewalls, load balancers, or storage to the end user. In our example, it is the drink or chips that makes it a meal.

There are also some basic ways in which a cloud can present its services to an end user, which are:

- **Private cloud**: A private cloud is sometimes referred to as an internal cloud. In other words, the cloud only exists within a business. The cloud consumes resources that are owned or operated by the business and only people that work for the organization can consume cloud resources. Examples are lab or development environments.

- **Public cloud**: A public cloud is sometimes called an external cloud. This means that an organization makes its cloud services available to the people outside of the organization. Examples are Amazon Cloud, iCloud, and so on.

- **Hybrid cloud**: A hybrid cloud, in the NIST definition, is exactly what you think it is—a mixture of a public and a private cloud. However, the IT community uses the term hybrid cloud to refer to a cloud interface that uses several different virtualization technologies to create the cloud. An example would be a cloud interface that can use VMware and Microsoft (Hyper-V) virtualization.

Now that you understand what a cloud can do, it doesn't come as a surprise that businesses want it, as it presents an opportunity to do the following:

- ✦ Offer self service to end customers: The cloud can present an easy-to-understand interface to end customers, enabling them to request services that would normally require the understanding of IT personnel

- ✦ Reduce IT overhead: Due to the self-serving nature of the cloud, the hands-on workload of IT personnel is reduced

- ✦ Deliver services to the end customer faster: Self-service and reduced involvement of IT-personnel results in faster delivery of services to the end customer

VMware Cloud

The VMware Cloud (also called vCloud) mainly provides PaaS and can be used to create private, public, and hybrid clouds (NIST definition). If you are wondering about the small "v" in front of most VMware products, it stands for VMware, or more recently, just for virtual. It's similar to the small "i" in front of Apple products.

The VMware Cloud's basic core is a product named VMware vCloud Director. It is an interface based on HTTPS (secure HTTP) that abstracts and presents the underlying virtualization for consumption to the end user. Basically, when we talk about the vCloud we are talking about VMware vCloud Director. It is the product that provides and manages the vCloud.

When we start talking about the vCloud, we need to understand that it actually describes a whole set of products that work together.

VMware vCloud Suite consists of the following base products working together; without all these components, the vCloud cannot exist:

+ **vSphere**: This describes the virtual infrastructure created by VMware products. It consists of the following products:
    ◦ **ESXi Servers**: They provide the base virtualization and make it possible for virtual machines (VMs) to exist. It presents resources (CPU, RAM networks, and storage) to the VMs for consumption.
    ◦ **VMware vCenter**: This manages ESXi Servers and their VMs. It is responsible for all the features such as clustering, vMotion, and VM templates.
+ **vCloud Networking and Security**: This (formally known as vShield) provides firewall, NAT, and isolated networks to the virtual infrastructure.
+ **VMware vCloud Director**: This glues all the previously mentioned products together to form the cloud.

These are the basic products that build the vCloud; however, VMware has some additional products that enrich the vCloud. These products are not essential but provide a lot of additional benefits.

+ **vCenter Operations Management**: This is an interface that lets you monitor your virtual environment and vCloud for performance and faults and also enables capacity planning
+ **vCloud Connector**: This provides methods to move VMs between vClouds
+ **VMware Chargeback**: This provides a method to measure the usage of virtual resources, create reports, and bills

People choose the VMware vCloud because VMware has a solid base (vSphere) on which the vCloud is built. Another reason is that there are a lot of extra products that support and enhance the vCloud. Enterprises choose VMware because of market saturation, support, and especially because it utilizes the already existing VMware investments. However, there are a lot of other products out there that use the underlying VMware vSphere to build a cloud without using VMware vCloud Director.

There has been considerable confusion in the past about what version of VMware goes with what. VMware cleared most of the confusion by aligning all the version numbers to 5.1 in its latest releases.

Visit the VMware Product Interoperability Matrixes (`http://partnerweb.vmware.com/comp_guide2/sim/interop_matrix.php`) to check compatibility. As for this book, we will be using the following versions:

+ VMware vCloud Director 5.1
+ VMware vCenter 5.1
+ VMware ESXi 5.1
+ VMware vCloud Networking and Security 5.1

Installation

In five steps, you can install vCloud Director and get it ready for use.

Step 1 – what do I need?

Before you install vCloud Director, you will have to prepare certain prerequisites, which will be laid out in this section.

You can find the full list of requirements in *vCloud Director Installation and Upgrade Guide*. This guide assumes that you have some minimal knowledge of either VMware Workstation or VMware vCenter.

Making a decision – appliance or full install

If you signed up for the VMware vCloud trial, you will have access to **vCloud Director Appliance**, which is designed to make your life easier as it is comes preconfigured and with an internal database. Sadly, the appliance doesn't work in VMware Workstation; therefore, you will find the installation of vCloud Director and vCloud Director Appliance in the *Step 4 – vCloud Director Appliance deployment* subsection.

- ✦ Use vCloud Director if you:
    - ○ Can download the `.bin` file from `www.vmware.com`
    - ○ Are using VMware Workstation
- ✦ Use vCloud Director Appliance if you:
    - ○ Are using a fully configured and working vCenter (not in Workstation)
    - ○ Have no access to the `.bin` file

A database

If you plan to use vCloud Director Appliance, you can skip this section.

vCloud Director supports either a Microsoft SQL (2005 or newer version) or an Oracle Database (11*g* or later version). The sizing is a bit unclear as VMware hasn't released a database sizing calculator for vSphere 5.1 or vCloud Director yet. For a lab environment, an initial size of 1 GB with auto expands and database owner (dbo) rights should see you through.

A Red Hat VM

If you plan to use vCloud Director Appliance, you can skip this step too.

vCloud Director is supported on **Red Hat Enterprise Linux** (**RHEL**) 64-bit, Version 5.4 to 6.2. Having said that, it also works on CentOS or SLES; however, VMware will not support this configuration.

The minimum configuration for the vCloud Director VM is two CPUs and 1 GB of memory with 5 GB of free disk space. More free space is recommended as it is also used for temporary storage of imports and exports. You can add more space for import, later, by mounting additional storage at /opt/vmware/vcloud-director/data/transfer.

A very important point is to provide two **Network Interface Cards** (**NICs**) as vCloud uses one NIC to spawn the HTTP interface and the other to accept VM console connections. A VM console connection allows you to use keyboard and mouse to interact with the VM.

Before you start installing vCloud Director Appliance, check to make sure that you have either disabled the firewall or allowed TCP port 443 for incoming connections. As a last step, we need to get the redhat-lsb package installed.

If you're not very familiar with Linux, I have included a small segment on how to build a Red Hat VM using VMware Workstation in *Step 2 – Downloading vCloud Director*.

A vSphere environment

As vCloud Director uses vSphere, we require an existing vSphere environment.

You should have the following ready and configured:

+ One vCenter Server 5.1 (including its SSO component)
+ One or more clusters with DRS enabled
+ One or more ESXi servers
+ Some free shared disk space

If you don't have sufficient hardware to install all these, you can install the vCenter Appliance and vESXi in VMware Workstation. With a bit of resizing, you can squeeze a whole vCD/vSphere environment onto an 8 GB laptop; however, don't expect much in terms of performance.

MyLab

In the following sections, we'll take a look at screenshots from the MyLab setup. To make it easier to understand the values you see in them, here is a quick peek into the MyLab setup.

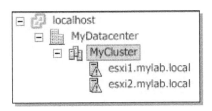

I configured **MyCluster** for DRS only, not HA. The ESXi servers (actually virtual ESXi on VMware Workstation) are vanilla builds and are connected to NFS shared storage, that is, they are not configured with storage DRS or storage profiles. With respect to network, I configured a Distributed vSwitch (DVS) with one port group for VMs but left the management and vMotion (same port group) on a normal vSwitch.

Domain Name	Network	Gateway	DNS
Mylab.local	192.168.220.0/24	192.168.220.02	192.168.220.02

The following table shows host name, IP address, and VM function:

Host name	IP address	VM function
Esxi1	192.168.220.05	vESXi
Esxi2	192.168.220.06	vESXi
ADSQL	192.168.220.11	Ad, SQL Server, DNS
vCenter	192.168.220.12	vCenter Appliance
vShield	192.168.220.13	vShield
vCD-http	192.168.220.14	vCD Appliance
vCD-console	192.168.220.15	

Some network considerations

Make sure that you have updated your DNS server with the IPs for vCenter, the ESXi hosts, and the two vCD IPs. A DNS server is not a must, but it makes things a little easier.

VMware vCloud Client

To access vCloud Director, you need a browser that is supported (currently, Safari is not) and you have to have Adobe Flash Player 11 installed. If you plan to upload or download files, you also need the latest version of Java.

If you are thinking of using an iPad, you will need to download the VMware vCloud Client app for iPad.

Step 2 – downloading vCloud Director

In this segment we will download all the components required to install vCloud.

Getting a trial license for vSuit

Browse to `http://www.vmware.com`, select **Products**, and choose **vCloud Director**.
On the vCloud Director site, you should find a button named **Download Free Trial**.

If you have a VMware account logon, you will receive a free 60-day trial version. If you don't have an account, you will have to create one.

Getting the software and keys

Download the following software from `http://www.vmware.com`:

  ✦ VMware vCloud Director or VMware vCloud Director Appliance
  ✦ VMware vCloud Networking and Security

On the same web page (or via your e-mail), you will receive a 60-day trial license key for vCloud Director and vCloud Networking and Security.

Step 3 – getting vCloud Networking and Security ready

When you downloaded the license key, you probably discovered that we are actually deploying vShield here, just with a new fancy name. I will use the old name as it's the name that is shown everywhere.

Let's get started with the deployment of Network and Security (vShield). It comes as a packaged VM called open virtualization appliance (OVA). Depending on whether you deploy it in Workstation or vCenter, the import is a little different.

Deploying a .ova template with vCenter

If you are using vCenter, click on **File** and select **Deploy OVF Template**.

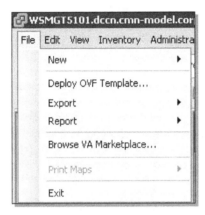

The import wizard will start up and ask you for the following information:

✦ Location of the template

✦ To accept the end user licensing agreement

✦ To specify the folder that the template should be installed in

✦ To specify the cluster and resource pool that the template should be installed in

✦ To specify the datastore where the template should be placed

✦ The setting for **Disk Format** (choose **Thick Provisioned Lazy Zeroed**)

✦ The name of the network the template should be attached to

✦ The setting for the **Power off after deploy** option (choose **Yes**)

Wait until the import has finished and the VM is powered on. Open the VM console.

Deploying a .ova template in VMware Workstation

If you are using VMware Workstation, simply double-click on the downloaded `.ova` file. The following pop up appears:

Enter the name (or just leave the default name) and choose the folder to store the template in. Click on **Import** and wait until the import is finished.

Depending on how you set up your network for your lab, you might need to change the network association of the VM. Also, if you are strapped for resources, you can pull the memory and CPU setting of the vShield VM down to 1 GB and one CPU.

Power the VM up and continue to the next part.

Login

After the VM has been deployed and powered on and the boot sequence has finished, you should see a prompt saying **Manager login**.

We now have to set the IP for this VM. To do that we have to log in and perform the following steps:

1. Log in with the username `admin` and the password `default`.
2. You should now see a prompt. Type `enable` and confirm again with the password `default`.
3. Type `setup` and the setup wizard will take you through the next steps.
4. Enter the IP address for this VM.
5. Enter the subnet mask for this VM.
6. Enter (or leave blank) the IP for the first DNS server.
7. Enter (or leave blank) the IP address for the secondary DNS server.
8. Enter (or leave blank) the Domain name.

9. Acknowledge with y if you typed everything correctly or with n if you made a mistake on the way.

```
Manager login: admin
Password:
Manager> enable
Password:
Manager# setup

Use CTRL-D to abort configuration dialog at any prompt.
Default settings are in square brackets '[]'.

IP Address (A.B.C.D): 192.168.220.13
Subnet Mask (A.B.C.D): 255.255.255.0
Default gateway (A.B.C.D): 192.168.220.2
Primary DNS IP (A.B.C.D): 192.168.220.11
Secondary DNS IP (A.B.C.D):
Warning: Secondary DNS not set.
DNS domain search list (space separated): mylab.local
Old configuration will be lost
Do you want to save new configuration (y/[n]): _
```

The vShield VM will take about 2 to 3 minutes to configure itself. Just wait a bit.

Register with vSphere Lookup Service and vCenter

Now we should be able to access the vShield web service by typing into your browser either the DNS name (if you registered it in your DNS server) or the IP address of the vShield VM.

You should now see a login screen, as follows:

Follow the ensuing steps:

1. Log in with the username `admin` and the password `default`. You should now see the main configuration screen.

2. Click on **Settings & Reports** and choose **Configuration** from the right-hand screen.

   Now we will register the vShield installation with the Lookup Service.

3. In the **Lookup Service** section, click on **Edit** on the right-hand side. A pop up will ask you for the following details:

   ° **Lookup Service Host**: This is the IP address or the hostname of the machine on which you installed SSO.

   ° **Port**: The port number should be 7444 (which is the default that it came with).

   ° **SSO Administrator or Username**: If you are using vCenter, your login should be `admin@System-Domain`. If you are using the vCenter Appliance, it will be `root`.

   ° **Password**: Enter the password for the account.

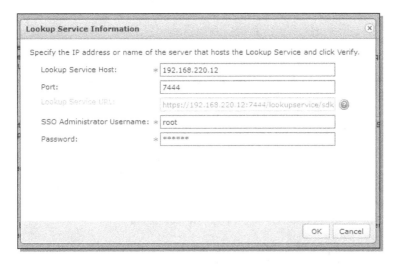

4. After successfully registering vShield with the lookup service, we now need to bind vShield to vCenter. Click on the **Edit** button on the right in the vCenter Server section. The pop up will ask for the following information:

  ° **vCenter Server**: vCenter Server name or IP address

  ° **Administrator Username**: The administrator account (if you are using the vCenter Appliance, it will be `root`)

  ° **Password**: Enter the password for the account

  ° Check the box **Assign vShield 'Enterprise Administrator' role to this user**

  ° Leave the other checkbox empty

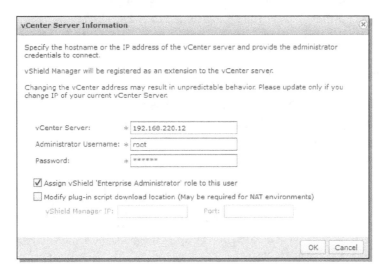

After this is done, vShield is configured and almost ready for use. We just need to license it.

Licence vShield

The licensing of vShield is done in vCenter and can only be performed after you have bonded vShield to vCenter.

In vCenter, navigate to **Home | Administration | Licensing**, enter the vShield license, and assign it to the vCloud Network and Security VM.

Step 4 – vCloud Director Appliance deployment

This section describes how to configure vCloud Director Appliance. If you have access to the `.bin` installation file for vCLoud Director, you can skip this part.

Deploying vCloud Director Appliance

Using the same method you used to import the vShield VM, you will now deploy vCloud Director Appliance.

After starting the OVF import wizard (**File | Deploy OVF Template**), the wizard will ask you for the following information:

+ The location of the template
+ To accept the end user licensing agreement
+ To specify the folder vCD should be installed in
+ To specify the cluster and resource pool vCD should be installed in
+ To specify the datastore in which vCD should be placed
+ The **Disk Format** (choose **Thick Provisioned Lazy Zeroed**)
+ The networks vCD should be attached to (choose the same for both and ignore the warning message)
+ To enter some more detailed information as follows:

    ○ What kind of database you are using (choose **Internal**)
    ○ Leave everything that refers to databases blank
    ○ In the **Network** section, enter:

        ○ **The Gateway address**
        ○ **The DNS server**
        ○ The IP address and network mask for the first network card (HTTP)
        ○ The IP address and network mask for the second network card (console)
        ○ **Power on after deploy** (choose **Yes**)

This will start the deployment process. Open a console and see it boot. The process will stop for a while at some stage, asking for a password; don't worry, just wait until it continues by itself.

After a while, the blue and white screen of a VMware appliance should make an appearance.

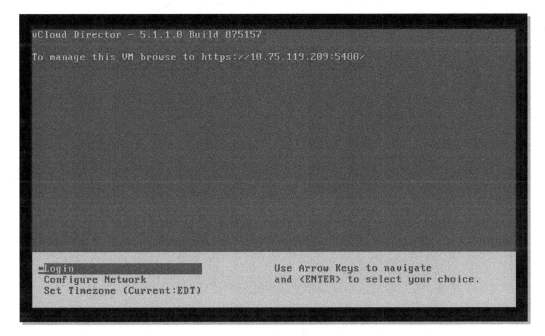

```
vCloud Director - 5.1.1.0 Build 875157

To manage this VM browse to https://10.75.119.209:5480/




 *Login                                Use Arrow Keys to navigate
  Configure Network                    and <ENTER> to select your choice.
  Set Timezone (Current:EDT)
```

You have successfully installed vCloud Director Appliance. Continue with the next step.

Step 5 – vCloud Director installation

If you have access to the `.bin` file for vCloud Director, this is how you install vCloud Director. If you have downloaded vCloud Director Appliance and configured it in the last step, ignore this part.

Creating a Red Hat VM

If you have limited Linux knowledge, the easiest way forward is to use VMware Workstation. Workstation has an easy install wizard that will do all the work for you and provide you with a running Red Hat VM.

Here is what you need to do:

1. Download the Red Hat Enterprise Linux 6.2 ISO from `www.redhat.com` (you can sign up for a 60-day trial).

2. In VMware Workstation, create a new VM, choose **Typical**, and use the downloaded ISO.

3. On the last page of the wizard, choose **Customize Hardware** and add a **Network Adapter**. Depending on your resources available, you may also want to increase the CPU count to two and memory to 2 GB.

4. Finish the wizard and sit back while the VM installs.

5. A graphical login screen should greet you. Log in with `root` (under **Others**) and the password you put previously into the wizard. Ignore the warnings and a screen similar to the Windows desktop should now be accessible to you. Note that the menu is on the upper border of the screen, not on the lower part (as in Windows).

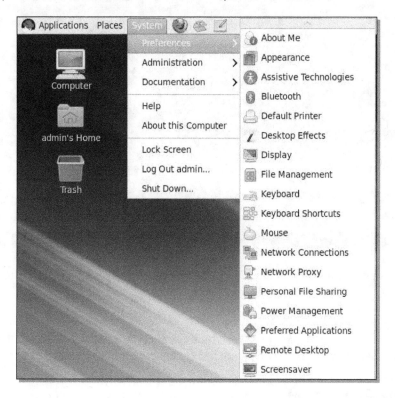

6. We now want to configure the Network cards. Choose **System | Preference | Network Connections**. (**eth0** is your first and **eth1** is your second network adapter.)

7. Set the **Method** field under the **IPv4 Settings** tab to **Manual** and then click on **Add**. Enter all the relevant information.

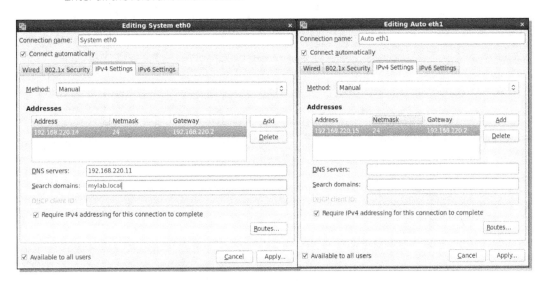

8. Now we need to disable the firewalls. Navigate to **System | Administration | Firewall**, and then click on the big red button **Disable**. Then, click on **Apply** and click on **Yes** in the dialog box showing the overwrite question.

The last major step is to install an additional software package.

1. First we need to connect the Workstation and the downloaded Red Hat ISO to the VM (CD-ROM).

2. Wait for a second until a new window pops up, showing the content of the CD-ROM.

3. Now navigate to **System | Administration | Add/Remove Software**.

4. In the search window next to the **Find** button, type in `lsb` and hit **Find**.

5. Four packages should be displayed. Check **LSB base libraries support for Red Hat Enterprise Linux** (with the line **redhat-lsb-4.0-3.el6 (x86_64)** under it). Click on **Apply** and acknowledge the other packages that need installing.

6. Wait until the installation is finished and close the window.

You have officially installed and configured a Red Hat Enterprise Linux VM.

In order to do the rest of the installation of vCloud Director, you need to open a terminal. Navigate to **Applications | System Tools | Terminal**. This will open a terminal where you can type the commands for the rest of the installation procedure.

Copying the .bin file to the vCD VM

There are several methods you can use for copying the .bin file to the vCD VM. If you are using VMware Workstation, use the shared folders, or SFTP or SCP. If all fails, create an ISO image with the file in it and mount it on the VM.

Use the cp command to copy the file to the /tmp folder. I used VMware Workstation shared folders, which mounts to c:\tmp on my computer.

```
cp /mnt/hgfs/tmp/vmware-vcloud-director-5.1.1-868405.bin /tmp
```

Executing the .bin file

The `.bin` file contains all the RPMs and other little scripts that are needed for the installation. In this step, only the RPM will be installed. No configuration will take place.

To make sure we can run the file in Linux, we need to make sure it's set to be executable. Use the `chmod` command to set the permissions.

```
chmod 555 /tmp/vmware-vcloud-director-5.1.1-868405.bin
```

Now let's execute the program.

```
/tmp/vmware-vcloud-director-5.1.1-868405.bin
```

Doing this will install the RPMs and will then ask you if you would like to run the configuration script. We don't want to run the script now. Enter `NO`.

Creating SSL certificates

Before we go to the actual installation of vCD, we need to create some SSL certificates. We need to create two certificates, one for the HTTP interface and one for the console interface of vCD.

The following commands will create a new JCE-based keystore for SSL certificates in `/opt/vmware/certificates.ks`. Create the SSL certificates using RSA encryption and assigning an alias to each of them.

Creating HTTP certificates

To create an HTTP certificate, use the following command:

```
/opt/vmware/vcloud-director/jre/bin/keytool -keystore /opt/vmware/certificates.ks -storetypeJCEKS -genkey -keyalgRSA -alias  http
```

Creating console certificates

To create a console certificate, use the following command:

```
/opt/vmware/vcloud-director/jre/bin/keytool -keystore /opt/vmware/certificates.ks -storetypeJCEKS -genkey -keyalgRSA -alias consoleproxy
```

When you run the commands, you will be asked several things. I have supplied some sample answers for each question. It is not really critical what answers you give, except if you want to use the created certificates to apply for a trusted certificate. If you mistype something, you can either say `No` at the end or simply delete the keystore and start over.

+ **Enter keystore password**: Define and confirm a password for the new keystore (confirming happens only the first time when you run the command), for example, P@ssw0rd.

+ **What is your first and last name?**: Here you enter the DNS name of the vCD VM, for example, vcd.mylab.local.

♦ **What is the name of your organizational unit?**: Enter what department of the organization vCD will be a part of, for example, IT.

♦ **What is the name of your organization?**: Enter the name of your organization, for example, MyCompany.

♦ **What is the name of your city or locality?**: Enter here the city or the data center your vCD lives in, for example, Melbourne.

♦ **What is the name of your state or province?**: Again, enter an appropriate location, for example, VIC.

♦ **What is the two-letter country code for this unit?**: Enter the two-letter code for your country, for example, AU. Find country codes at http://en.wikipedia.org/wiki/ISO_3166-1_alpha-2.

♦ **Is CN=vcd.mylab.local, OU=IT, O=MyCompany, L=Melbourne, ST=VIC, C=AU correct?**: Are the answers you gave correct? Enter yes or no.

♦ **Enter key password for <http>**: Define and confirm a password for this key. The password for the keys can be the same as for the keystore, for example, P@ssw0rd.

After you run both scripts, we are finally ready to get vCD up and running.

Running the configuration script

Now, we are running the vCD configuration script that will install and connect vCD to a database and start the vCD service.

The command to start the script is:

```
/opt/vmware/vcloud-director/bin/configure
```

The script will ask you the following questions. As before, find my sample answers after each question.

♦ Choose the network card that should be used with the HTTP interface:

```
Please enter your choice for the HTTP service IP address:
        1. 192.168.220.14
        2. 192.168.220.15
Choice [default=1]: 1
```

♦ Choose the network card that should be used for the consoles:

```
Please enter your choice for the remote console proxy IP address:
        1. 192.168.220.15
Choice [default=1]:1
```

✦ Enter the path to the SSL keystore:

```
Please enter the path to the Java keystore containing your SSL
certificates and private keys:/opt/vmware/certificates.ks
```

You will be prompted for the password.

✦ We won't configure syslog servers for this installation. You can skip this part by pressing *Enter*:

```
Syslog host name or IP address [press Enter to skip]:
```

✦ Choose what database you are using:

```
The following database types are supported:
        1. Oracle
        2. Microsoft SQL Server
Enter the database type [default=1]:2
```

✦ Now, enter the database connection variables. Depending on what database you choose, the questions differ slightly.

Microsoft SQL Server	Oracle
`Enter the host (or IP address) for the database:myDB.mylab. local`	`Enter the host (or IP address) for the database:myDB.mylab.local`
`Enter the database port [default=1433]:`	`Enter the database port [default=1521]:`
Press *Enter* and you should see the following output:	Press *Enter* and you should see the following output:
`Using default value "1433" for port.`	`Using default value "1521" for port.`
`Enter the database name [default=vcloud]:vCloud`	`Enter the database service name [default=orcl]:vCDDB1AT`
`Enter the database instance [Press enter to use the server's default instance]:`	
`Press Enter`	
`Enter the database username:u_ vcd`	`Enter the database username:u_vcd`
`Enter the database password:P@ ssw0rd`	`Enter the database password:P@ ssw0rd`

After entering all the data, vCD will connect to the database and start creating some tables and fill them up with information. If the connection doesn't work, the script will take you back to choose a database.

♦ We let the configuration script start our vCD service when we enter y at the following prompt:

```
Do you want to start vCloud Director
Start it now? [y/n] y
```

Step 6 – setting up the vCloud Director Setup wizard

Now that we have finished installing the Linux component of vCloud Director, we will use the vCloud Director setup wizard. If you are using vCloud Director Appliance, you will also need to follow these instructions.

Accessing the web client

Now that vCD is installed, we need to finish some last steps to get it working and ready for action.

Open your browser—whether Internet Explorer, Firefox, or Chrome—and enter the following:

```
https://vcd.mylab.local.
```

Assuming your DNS is working, this should bring you to vCloud Director and show you a welcome screen for the **VMware vCloud Director Setup** wizard. If your DNS doesn't work, try the following IP address:

```
https://192.168.220.14
```

Running the setup wizard

The wizard will guide you through the process of finalizing the setup of vCD. It will ask you to:

1. Accept the licensing agreement. Read it and simply accept it.

2. Enter your vCloud Director licensing key, which you received earlier in the *Step 2 – downloading vCloud Director* section. Define an Administrator user.

3. This will create a user that exists only inside vCD. You will have to fill out all the fields. If you don't have a mail server in your setup, don't worry; just add a bogus address as shown in the previous screenshot.

4. Don't forget the password, or else you won't be able to log in.

5. Give your vCD installation a name and ID.

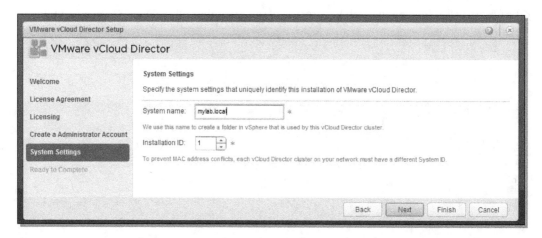

The name and the ID is used to identify individual vCDs when multiple vCDs are present. If you only have one vCD, it doesn't matter what you put in there. However, the name of the system and its ID is fixed after this step.

6. The finish screen will show a summary of the settings you entered. Just click on finish.

Open for business

vCD should now reload the page and present you with a login screen. Log in with the username you created in the wizard.

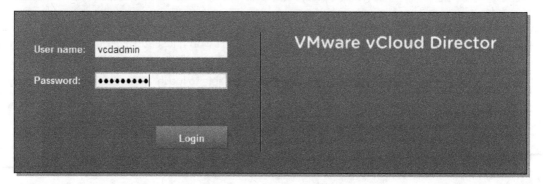

After all this, vCD should present you with the following screen:

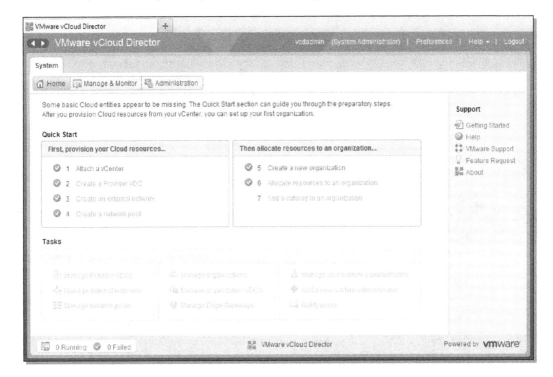

And that's it!

By this point, you should have a working installation of VMware vCloud Director 5.1.1 and are free to play around and discover more about it.

Quick start – creating your first VM

Now that we have vCloud Director installed, we can start playing with it. Our first aim is obviously to deploy a VM inside our vCloud. To do that, we have to assign resources (CPU memory, and disk) to vCD for consumption. In step 1 we will learn about all the different types of resources, and in steps 2 to 5, we will build them. Step 6 finally builds a vApp. Last but not least, I will give you some ideas about what to explore next.

Step 1 – understanding vCloud resources

This step will introduce you to how resources work in vCloud Director. The following diagram shows how resources are managed in vCloud and how they work together. The diagram is simplified and doesn't show all the vCloud properties; however, it is sufficient to explain the resource design.

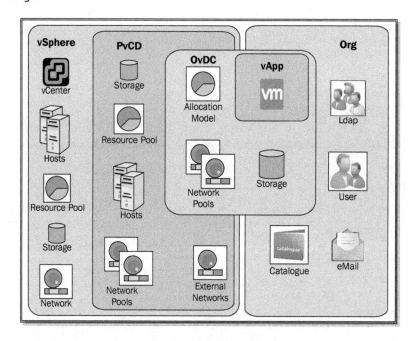

PvDC

A Provider Virtual Data Center (PvDC) represents a portion of all the virtual resources of a vSphere environment. It will take all the CPU and memory resources from a given resource pool or cluster and present them to the vCloud as consumable resources. A typical cluster or resource pool contains multiple datastores, storage profiles, and networks as well as multiple hosts. A PvDC will automatically gain access to these resources. It is basically the link between vSphere and the vCloud world.

Org

An **organization (Org)** is a container that holds users and groups and regulates their access to the vCloud resources. Users can be either locally created or imported from **Lightweight Directory Access Protocol (LDAP)** or **Active Directory (AD)**; however, groups can only be imported.

It is possible to assign different LDAP, e-mail, and notification settings to each organization. This is one of the most powerful features of vCloud Director. Its usage becomes clear if you think about a public cloud model. You could link different organizations into the different customers' LDAP/AD and e-mail systems (assuming a VPN tunnel between vCloud and the customer network), extending the customer's sphere of influence into the cloud. If a customer doesn't have or doesn't want to use his / her own LDAP/AD, he / she could make use of the local user function.

OvDC

An Organizational Virtual Data Center (OvDC) is a mixture of an Org with a PvDC. The Org defines who can do what and the PvDC defines where it is happening. Each OvDC is assigned one of the three allocation models as well as storage profiles.

The three allocation models are designed to provide different methods of resource allocation. Let's first look at the difference between the models:

+ **Reservation pool**: This allocates a fixed amount of resources (in GHz and GB) from the PvDC to the OvDC. This model is good if the users want to define a per-VM resource allocation. Only this model enables the **Resource Allocation** tab in VMs.

+ **Allocation pool**: This is similar to reservation pool; however, you can also assign how many resources are guaranteed (reserved) for this OvDC. This model is good for overcommitting resources.

+ **Pay-as-you-go (PAYG)**: This is similar to the allocation pool; however, recourses are only consumed if vApps/VMs are running. All other models reserve resources even if the OvDC doesn't contain any running VMs. This model is useful if the number of resources is unknown or fluctuating.

There are different settings that one can choose from for each model.

	Allocation Pool	PAYG	Reservation Pool
CPU allocation (GHz)	Yes	Yes and unlimited	Yes
CPU resources guaranteed (percentage)	Yes	Yes	N/A
vCPU max speed (Ghz)	Yes	Yes	N/A

	Allocation Pool	PAYG	Reservation Pool
Memory allocation (GB)	Yes	Yes and unlimited	Yes
Memory resources guaranteed (percentage)	Yes	Yes	N/A
Maximum number of VMs (number or unlimited)	Yes	Yes	Yes

vApp

You might have encountered the name before in vCenter; however, the vApp of vCD and the vApp of vCenter are totally different beasts. vApps in vCenter are essentially resource pools with extras, such as a startup sequence. A vApp in vCD is a container that exists only in vCD. However, it can also contain isolated networks and allows the configuration of a start-and-stop sequence for its member VMs. In addition to all this, you can allow this vApp to be shared with other members of your organization.

VM

The most atomic part of a vCD is the VM. VMs live in vApps. Here you can configure all the settings you are familiar with from vSphere, and some more. You are able to add/update/delete vHardware as well as define guest customization.

Step 2 – connecting vCenter to vCD

Let's start with the process of assigning resources to the vCloud. The first step is to assign a vCenter to this vCD installation. For future reference, one vCD installation can use multiple vCenters.

As a starting point for steps 2 to 5, we will use the home screen, as shown in the following screenshot:

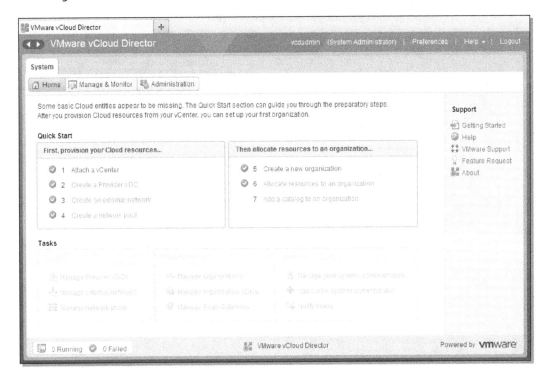

1. On the **Home** screen (or if you like, the welcome screen), click on the first link, **Attach a vCenter**.

2. A pop up will ask you for the following details for your vCenter:

    ○   **Host name or IP address**: Enter the fully qualified domain name (FQDN) or IP address of your vCenter

    ○   **Port number**: Port 443 is the correct default port

    ○   **User name** and **Password**: Enter the username and password of an account that has administrator rights in vCenter

    ○   **vCenter name**: Give your vCenter a name with which you would like to identify it in vCloud

- Description: A description isn't required; however, it doesn't hurt either
- vSphere Web Client URL: Now enter the URL for the web vCenter client — `https://(FDQN or IP)/vsphere-client`

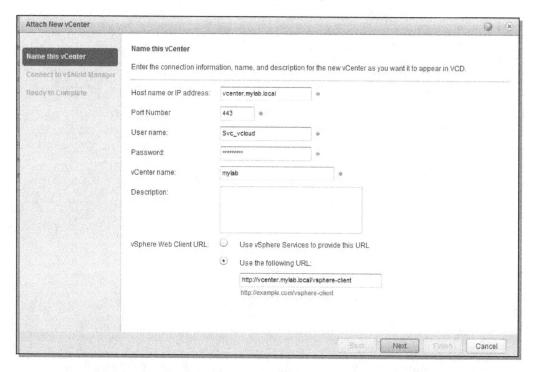

3. After vCD has accepted the information and contacted vCenter, we now need to enter all the details for the vShield installation (from the *Step 2 – downloading vCloud Director* subsection in the *Installation* section).

   - Enter the FQDN or IP address of the vShield VM
   - And if you didn't change the default password, you can log in with `admin` as ID and `default` as the password

4. vCD contacts vShield and that's that.

You have now connected vCD to vCenter and are now able to use resources presented by this vCenter in your vCloud.

Step 3 – creating a PvDC

Now we will create our first PvDC and assign resources to our vCloud.

1. To create a new PvDC, you click on the second link, **Create a Provider VDC** (refer to the first image in the *Step 2 – connecting vCenter to vCD* subsection of the *Quick start – creating your first VM* section).

2. Enter a name for the new PvCD. A good idea is to develop a naming standard for any item in vCenter and vCD. My PvDC will be called `PvDC_myLab`.

3. Choose the highest supported virtual hardware version that your vCenter/ESXi supports. If you are running VMware 5.1, it is Version 9.

4. In the next window, we choose the cluster or the resource pool that vCloud should use to create the PvDC. Please note that you need to create a resource pool before starting this wizard, or else it won't show up. For this example, I choose the cluster `myCluster`.

5. In the next window, we are prompted to choose a storage profile. For the time being, just choose any and continue.

6. Now vCD shows us all the ESXi hosts that belong to the cluster or the resource pool we selected. vCD will need to install some extra software on them and will need to connect directly to the ESXi hosts. That's why it is asking for the credentials of the ESXi hosts.

7. Finish the wizard.

At the end of this wizard, vCD will put the ESXi into maintenance mode to install the extra software package. If you only have one ESXi host and it is also running vCD and vCenter, you will have to manually install the vCD software package (not in the scope of this book).

You have now successfully carved off a slice of resources to be used inside your vCloud.

Storage profiles

vSphere storage profiles are defined in vCenter. The idea is to group datastores together by their capabilities or by a user-defined label. For example, group datstores by their types (NFS, Fiber, SATA, or SSD), different RAID types, or by features that are provided, such as backup or replication.

Enterprises use storage profiles such as gold, silver, and bronze, depending on the speed of the disks (SATA or SSD) and on whether a datastore is backed up or replicated for DR purposes.

vCloud Director can assign different storage profiles to PvDCs and OvDCs. If an OvDC has multiple storage profiles assigned to it, you can choose a specific storage profile to be the default for this OvDC. Also, when you create a vApp in this OvDC, you can choose the storage profile with which you want to store the vApp.

Step 4 – creating an Org

And now we will create an organization (Org).

1. On the **Home** panel, click on the fifth link, **Create a new organization** (refer to the first image in the *Step 2 – connecting vCenter to vCD* subsection of the *Quick start – creating your first VM* section).

2. Give the Org a name, for example, MyOrg and the organization's full name.

3. In the next window, choose the first option, **Do not use LDAP**.

4. Next, we could add a local user but we won't. So let's just click on **Next**.

5. Our first Org should be able to share. So click on **Allow publishing...**, and then click on **Next**.

6. We keep clicking on **Next**. The first Org will use the e-mail and notification settings of vCD.

7. Now we need to configure the leases. You can just click on **Next**, or if you like, set all leases to **unlimited**.

8. The last window shows us all the settings we have selected, and by clicking on **Finish**, our first organization will be created.

System Org

You have actually created a second Org as the first Org is called system and was created when we installed vCD. If you look at your home screen, you will see that there is a small tab that says **System**. The system Org is the mother of all Orgs. It's where other Orgs, PvDCs, OvDCs, and basically all settings are defined in vCloud Director. The system organization can only be accessed by vCloud system administrators.

Step 5 – creating an OvDC

Now that we have our first Org, we can proceed with assigning resources to it for consumption. To do that, we need to create an Organization Virtual Data Center (OvDC).

1. On the **Home** Screen, we click on the sixth link, **Allocate resources to an organization**.

2. First we have to select the Org to which we want to assign the resources. As we only have one Org, the choice is easy.

3. Next, we are asked which PvDC we want to take the resources from. Again, we only have one PvDC, so we choose that one. Note that the screen shows you what percentage of various resources of this PvDC are already committed and which networks are associated with this PvDC. Don't be alarmed that no networks are showing; we haven't configured any yet.

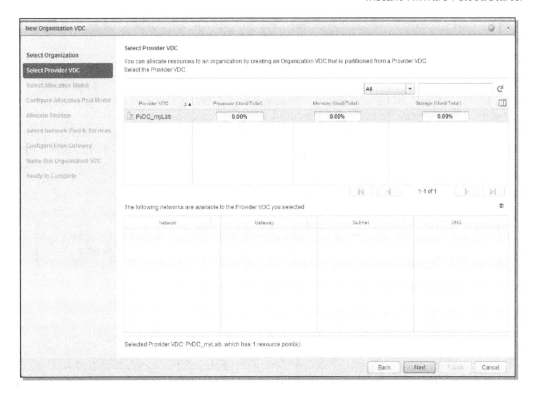

4. Next we choose the allocation model. We have discussed the details of all the three models earlier: allocation pool, pay-as-you-go, and reservation pool.

5. Choose **Pay-as-you-go** and click on **Next**. Have a look at the settings and click on **Next**.

6. The next window lets you define which storage profile you would like to use for this OvDC. If you don't have a storage profile configured (as I do in my lab), just select any and click on the **Add** button.

   ° Enable **Thin Provisioning** to save on storage. This setting is the same as the normal thin provisioning in vSpere.

   ° Enable **Fast Provisioning**. This setting will use vCloud-linked clones (explained later).

7. This window lets us configure the network resources for the organization. As we haven't configured any networking yet, just click on **Next**. We will discuss the network options in the next section about networks.

8. We don't want to create an edge gateway so we leave the setting as it is and click **Next**. Again, more information about this is to follow in the next section.

9. Finally, we will give this OvDC a name and finish the creation. I normally add a little descriptor in the name to say what allocation model I used, for example, res, payg, or allo.

We have now successfully assigned memory, CPU, and storage to be consumed by our organization.

Linked clones

Linked clones save an enormous amount of storage space. When a VM is created from a template, a full clone of the template is created. When linked clones are used, only the changes to the VM are written to disk. As an example, we have a VM with 40 GB storage capacity (ignore thin provisioning for this example). A full clone would need another 40 GB of disk space. If linked clones are used, only a few MB will be used. As more changes are made to the cloned VM, it will demand more storage (up to the maximum of 40 GB). If this reminds you of the way snapshots work in vSphere, that's because that is what is actually used in the background.

 vCloud linked clones are not the same technology as VMware View linked clones; they are a more advanced version of the VMware Lab Manager linked clones.

Step 6 – creating a vApp

Now that we have resources within our organization, we can create a vAPP and the VM inside it.

vApps are created inside organizations, so we first need to access the organization that was created in the *Step 4 – creating an Org* subsection of the *Quick start – creating your first VM* section.

1. Click on the **Manage & Monitor** tab and double-click on the **Organizations** menu item.

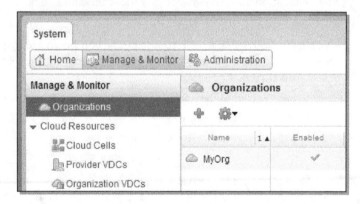

2. Now double-click on the organization we created in the *Step 4 – creating an Org* subsection of the *Quick start – creating your first VM* section. You will see that a new tab is opened with the name of the new Org. You are now on the home screen of this Org.

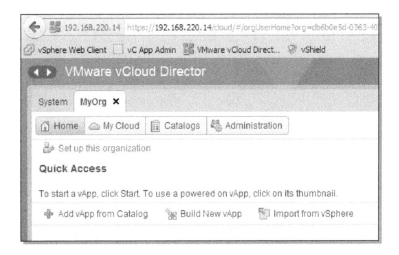

3. We will take the easy road here. Click on **Build New vApp**.

4. Give your first vApp a name (for example, `MyFirstVapp`), a description, and if you like, explore the settings of the leases.

5. After you click on **Next,** we are asked to choose a template. As we currently don't have one, we click on **New Virtual Machine** in the left-hand side menu of the screen. We will learn about templates in the *Top features you need to know about* section.

6. A pop up will appear and we will then select all the settings we would expect when creating a new VM, such as name and hostname, CPU, memory, OS type and version, hard disk, and network. Note that if you are using virtual ESXi servers in your lab, you may be limited to 32-bit VMs only.

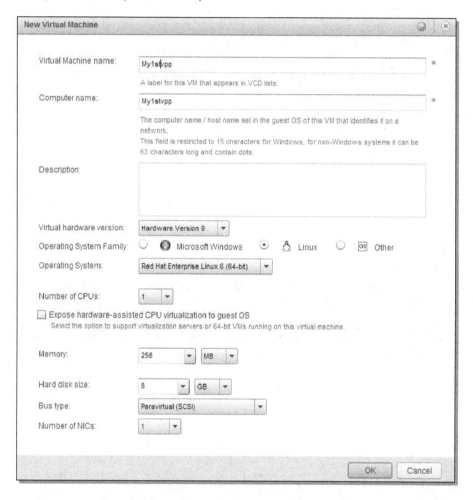

7. After clicking on **OK,** we will find ourselves back at the previous screen. However, our VM should now show up in the lower table. Click on **Next.**

8. We can now choose in which OvDC and in what storage profile we will deploy the vApp. The choices should be very limited at the moment, so just click on **Next.**

9. Next, we are asked to choose a network. As we don't have one, we just click on **Next**.

10. Another window will open; click on **Next**. Normally, we could define a fencing here.

11. At last, we see a summary of all the settings, and clicking on **Finish** will create our first vApp.

After the vApp is created, you can power it on and have a closer look.

1. Click on the play button to power the vApp on.

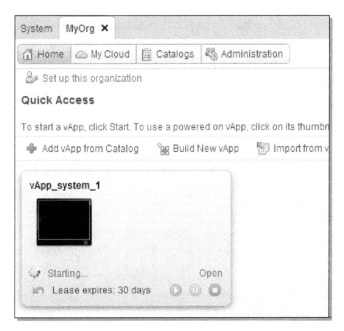

2. Wait for a few seconds, and then click on the black screen of the VM. A console pop up should come up and show you the BIOS of the booting VM. If that's not happening, check your browser security settings.

That's it! You have installed vCD, and you've configured your resources and created your first vApp.

Go and explore

In the previous steps, we had to gloss over some of the other features of vCloud Director to stay within the limits of this book. We will continue in the next section with some basic operations. However, I would encourage you to go and explore. Have a look at these exploring suggestions:

- In the system organization, check out all the menu items in **Manage and Monitor**. If you followed our example, you should find an error. Can you find it?

> In the network pool, the VXLAN network pool could not be created because we didn't enable it in the vShield.

- In the system organization, explore the **Administration** menu points.
- In the "real" organization, check out the various settings.
- Explore what this section has done to your vCenter.
- Check the property of a VM and see how the ID relates to the name in vCenter.
- Create new Orgs and OvDCs. Check how it affects vCenter.
- Create some new vApps and delete them. Check how it affects vCenter.
- Add and delete some VMs from a vApp. Check how it affects vCenter.
- Use the VM console to connect an ISO (for example, the Red Hat one from the *Step 5 – vCloud Director installation* subsection of the *Installation* section) and install an OS in the VM.

In the network pool, the VXLAN network pool could not be created because we didn't enable it in the vShield.

Top 2 features you'll want to know about

As you start to use vCloud Director, you will realize that there are a wide variety of things that you can do with it. This section will focus on the most powerful functions that vCloud Director has to offer: templates and networks.

Catalog, media, and templates

In the last section, we created our first vApp, and if you went exploring, you might have been able to install an operating system on the VM. In this segment, we will look a bit more into how to import ISO files as well as create and use templates.

In this section, we will work inside our organization that we created in the *Step 4 – creating an Org* subsection of the *Quick start – creating your first VM* section.

To access an organization, perform the following steps:

1. From the system organization, click on **Manage & Monitor**.

2. Click on **Organizations**.

3. Double-click on the Org you would like to work with (for example, MyOrg).

Creating a catalog

Before we can create vApp templates or use media, we have to create a catalog. A catalog is a storage unit for vApp templates and media. Media here basically means CD-ROM (.iso) or floppy (.flp) images.

1. To create a new catalog, we first need to access the organization.

2. Now click on **Catalogs**.

3. Click on the green + icon.

4. In the pop-up window, enter a name for the new catalog (for example, My Cat).

5. For now, leave the shares as they are—empty. Click on **Next**.

6. Now we are asked if we want to share the catalog; select **Publish to all organizations**. Note that, if this option doesn't show up, you may not have allowed for shared catalogs in the previous section, where we created the Org.

7. Click on **Finish**.

So now you have a new catalog and we are ready to import a media file into it. As we have enabled sharing for catalogs when we create the organization, we will be able to access the uploaded media files from any other organizations.

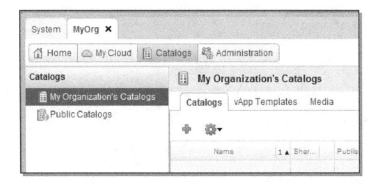

 You can set up an Org (PAYG) with a shared catalog that is only there to publish media files and templates. This Org is owned by the IT team and makes sure that only the standardized templates are used in all other Orgs.

Media

Media comprises basically of CD-ROM or floppy images. Nowadays we can safely ignore floppy images, so let's upload an ISO file. If you don't have an ISO file, you can download several Linux-based ones from the Internet, or you can reuse the Red Hat one we worked with in the *Step 5 – vCloud Director installation* subsection of the *Installation* section.

Upload media

You can either import media from vSphere or upload one. We will upload an ISO file in this example.

1. Click on the catalog that you've created.

2. There are now two tabs, **vApp Templates** and **Media**. Click on **Media**.

3. The first two icons are for uploading and importing. We select the first one, which looks like a hard disk.

4. Another pop up will appear, maybe accompanied by some Java messages asking if it's ok to run the app, which it is.

5. Browse to the file you would like to upload and give it a name under which it will appear in the catalog.

6. Click on **Upload**. Another pop up appears and asks you to accept the certificate of your vCD installation. Just click on **Yes** and the upload should now work.

7. After the upload is finished, you have your first media file in your catalog.

By uploading and sharing the typical ISOs (Windows, Linux, or applications) users are able to use them in their own VMs.

Working with media

Now that we have an ISO image in our catalog, we can (if you didn't already do so) install the operating system. To do this, we need to insert our ISO file into the virtual CD-ROM of the VM.

1. In your Org, Click on **My Cloud**.

2. Click on the vApp you have created in the *Step 6 – creating a vApp* subsection of the *Quick start – creating your first VM* section (or create a fresh one). This should open up the vApp and show you the VMs contained in the vApp.

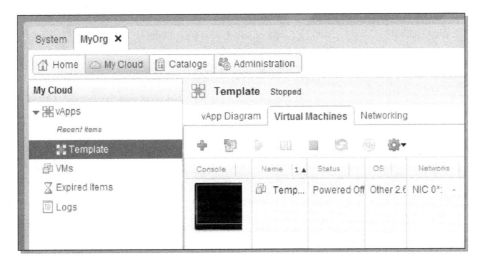

3. Right-click on the VM and select **Insert CD/DVD from Catalog.**

4. Select the ISO image that you have uploaded and click on **Insert**.

5. Power on the VM by clicking on the VM screen.

6. Your browser will now prompt you to install the plugin for the remote desktop, which might include closing your browser. Finish that process and navigate back to this step.

7. The console should now show you the VM desktop from the CD.

8. We want to make a template in the next segment from this VM, so installing an operating system is recommended.

9. When you are finished, you can eject the ISO file using the same right-click you used before; this time just select **Eject CD/DVD**.

For the network section of this book, it is a good idea to have a Linux and a Windows VM ready in two different vApps. It is not absolutely necessary to have both OS types; however, it helps a lot with playing with vCD. You don't have to build them from scratch; you are welcome to import them from vSphere.

vApp template

Now that we have a VM with an OS and a catalog, we can create a vApp template. A vApp template is basically the same as a conventional vSphere template, including guest customization. However, a vSphere template is only one VM, while a vCD vApp template can be a collection of VMs, their networks, and even their firewall rules.

First we will create a simple one-VM vApp template, then we will go into how to use templates, and finally, we will talk about the customization of templates.

Creating a vApp template

The creation of a vApp template starts with a vApp. We created a one-VM vApp in the previous segments, and now it is time to make a template out of it. It is a quite a straightforward process.

1. We start with the vApp. Click on **My Cloud**. You should now see the vApps you have created.

2. Make sure the vApp is stopped (just press the stop button and wait until the status shows **Stopped**).

3. Right-click on a vApp you would like to have a template of, and select **Add to Catalog...**.

4. The pop up will allow you to define a name for the template and a description. More importantly, you can define the OvDC, the storage profile, and the catalog the template should be stored in as well as the storage lease.

5. The last setting on this page is whether you want customization to happen when the VM template is deployed or not. We will look into the customization a bit later, but for now, just select **Customize VM settings**.

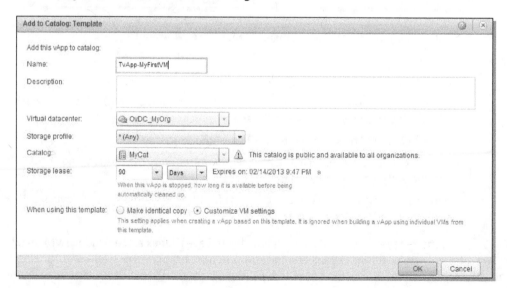

6. After clicking on **OK,** the vApp will show busy for some time. After it's back to **Stopped,** make your way back to the catalog you have created.

7. You should now have a template in it.

There are two types of templates, the normal template and the gold template. Basically a gold template is not different from any other template; however, it has the gold flag. We will now create a golden template.

1. Repeat the previous process and create another template of the same vApp; just make sure you give it another name.

2. After the new template shows in the catalog, right-click on it and select **Properties**.

3. Set **Gold Master** to **Yes** and click **OK**.

4. Looking into your catalog, you will see that the template we have been working on shows a gold disk symbol.

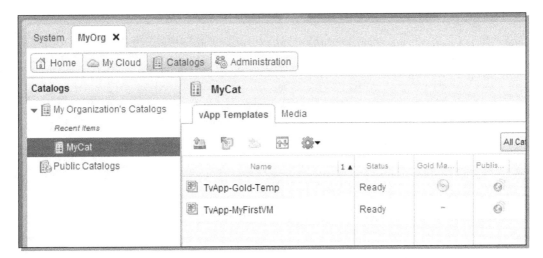

The difference between a normal template and a gold template will be seen in the next part when we deploy a template.

As of the writing of this book, there is a bug in the guest customization for Windows. Check out *VMware Knowledge Base article number 2038286.* See also the *People and places you should get to know* section for VMware support. This bug will not impact you for the examples in this book.

Deploying vApp templates

Now that we have vApp templates, we will deploy them.

1. Go back to the organization's **Home** screen.

2. Click on the green **+** icon (tooltip: **Add vApp from Catalog**).

3. The pop-up will show you the gold template. If nothing shows, that's probably due to the fact that you are in a different organization than the one you have created the template in. Select from the **Look in** drop-down menu **Published catalogs**.

4. Click on **All Templates**. You now should see both the templates. That is basically the difference between a gold and a normal template.

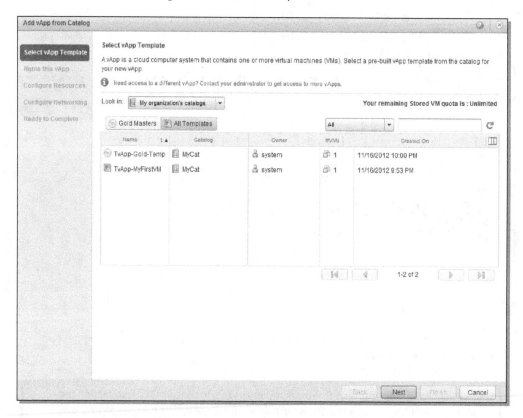

5. Select one of the templates and click on **Next**.

6. Give the new vApp a name and click on **Next**.

7. In this window, we can now choose the OvDC and the storage profile where the new vApp should live. But more importantly, we define a name for the VM inside the vApp. The default name is the name of the VM template. Make sure you change the VM name for this example.

8. Next you choose the hostname of the new VM; again, the default is the hostname of the template. Make sure you change the hostname to a new name for this example. Additionally we can choose the network the VM should be connected to; however, we don't have a network yet, so just click on **Next**. We will deal with networks extensively in the *Networks* section ahead.

9. After clicking on **Next**, we see all the settings we have chosen, and on the lower-left corner, we are able to select automatic power on after creation.

10. After the vApp has been deployed, power on the VM.

11. Watch the boot sequence of the VM. If the VM is a Windows VM, you will need to have a bit more patience. What basically happens here is that the VM boots up, guest customization happens, and then a final reboot occurs. After the final reboot, the hostname and (later) the network settings will have changed. Have a look!

You now know how to deploy a VM from a template. We will use this knowledge in the steps to follow.

 Use gold templates to mark templates as standardized business-approved templates.

Configuring customization of vApp templates

Now that we know the basics about templates, we can start with customization. Customization of templates actually starts in the vApp, not the template. This means that all the settings we want customized need to be done before we add the vApp to the catalog.

Let's have a look at which settings are customizable.

1. Click through to the VM you would like to customize.

2. Right-click on it and choose **Properties**.

3. If you haven't been here before, take some time and have a look around.

4. For customization, we go to **Guest OS Customization**. The **Guest OS Customization** window allows us to:

    ◦ Enable guest OS customization.

    ◦ Change the SID of a Windows system (Windows only).

    ◦ Reset the administrator (root) password to an auto-generated one (which shows up here later) or to a pre-set one. This requires the admin to set a new password on the first login.

    ◦ Automatically join the VM to an AD domain (Windows only).

    ◦ Run the script in the OS after boot. The script can be of any language that the OS understands. For example, DOS commands, powershell, and bash.

The ability to run a script is extremely powerful as it allows you to run additional customization inside the operating system.

 If you use a Windows system older than Windows 2008 or Vista, you need to install the Windows sysprep files in vCD.

Now we want to use the customization settings. Starting from where we left off:

1. Enable guest OS customization and change the administrator or root password.

2. Depending on the OS type you are running, put the following lines into the customization script field. This mini-script will write a file called Test.txt into the directory of the VM that contains its network information.

Windows	Linux
`ipconfig /all > c:\test.txt`	`/sbin/ifconfig> /tmp/test.txt`

3. Now click on **OK** and exit **Properties**.

4. Now proceed with making the vApp a template as you have learned earlier.

5. Deploy the template and power it on.

6. Check out the change of password (remember, Windows needs a bit more time to fire guest customization up).

7. Check out the content of the Test.txt file. We will do that later again when we actually have a network to play with, but there should still be some content.

And that's it! Remember that a vApp template can contain not only one VM, but a whole environment. You are now able to prepare a whole environment for rapid deployment. Now think how this could improve the development of multitiered applications.

Networks

Now that you have some basic techniques, let's look at Networks.

There are basically three kinds of networks in a vCloud: vApp, Org, and external networks. We will discuss the different kinds of networks as we go along.

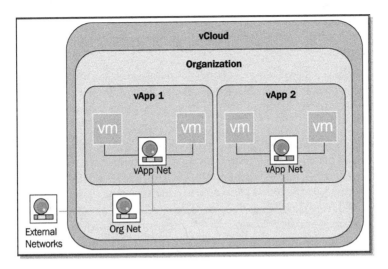

+ A **vApp network** is a network that only exists inside a vApp. You can have multiple vApp networks inside one vApp. A vApp network can connect to VMs and to Org networks.

+ An **organization network (Org Net)** is a network that exists only inside organizations. You can have multiple Org Nets in an organization. They can connect to VMs, vApp networks, and external networks.

+ An **external network** is a network that exists outside the vCloud, for example, a production network. External networks can only connect to Org networks.

We will build a vApp network, directly connected Org Net and an external network. However, after completing this part, you should be able to create the other versions yourself.

 You can replicate your production network as a vApp network, connecting it to your real production network with an Org Net providing an air gap between them.

Network pools

Before we can start creating and using any networks, we need to define at least one network pool. For vCloud to create a vApp or Org network, we need a Layer 2 isolated network (for example, VLAN isolated) that exists between the ESXi servers, basically, a VLAN that is trunked only to the ESXi servers. Network pools can be shared between the organizations. There are four kinds of network pools that can be created.

+ **VXLAN**: VXLAN networks are Layer 2 networks that are encapsulated in Layer 3 packages. VMware calls this Software Defined Networking (SDN). VXLANs are automatically created by vCD; however, they don't work out of the box and require some extra configuration in vShield (see the *People and places you should get to know* section).

- ✦ **vSphere portgroup backed**: vCD will use precreated portgroups to build the vApp or organization networks. You need to preprovision one portgroup for every vApp / organization network you would like to use.

- ✦ **VLAN-backed**: vCD will use a pool of VLAN numbers to automatically provision portgroups on demand; however, you still need to configure the VLAN trunking. You will need to reserve one VLAN for every vApp / organization network you would like to use.

- ✦ **Network isolation-backed**: These are the same as VXLANs; however, they work out of the box. The difference is that VXLAN can transcend routers and network isolation-backed networks can't. vCD uses one VLAN to create multiple isolated networks. You need to trunk the VLAN you would like to use and increase the MTU to 1,600, as additional information needs to be encapsulated into the network package. Network isolation-backed pools only support VMware distributed vSwitches.

VXLANs and network isolation networks solve the problems of preprovisioning and reserving a multitude of VLANs, which makes them extremely important.

Creating a network isolated pool

Here we will create a network isolation-backed network pool. However I would encourage you to try out the other versions later.

1. Please make sure that the VLAN you are using for the network pool is trunked to all ESXi hosts and that it is not used by anything else.

2. In the system organization, we click on **Manage & Monitor** and then on **Network Pools**.

3. Now click on the green **+** icon to **add a network pool**.

4. Select **Network Isolation-backed**.

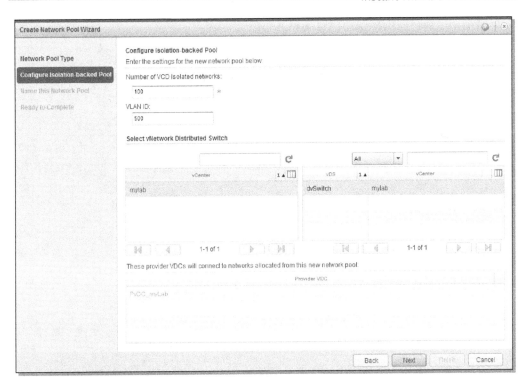

5. Define how many networks you would like to create. The maximum is 1,000.

6. Type in the VLAN number you would like to use for the network pool.

7. Now select the vCenter and the distributed switch you want to use.

8. Give the network pool a name.

9. After clicking on **Next,** you will see all the values you have entered.

10. Click on **Finish** in order to create the network pool.

Assigning a network pool to an OvDC

Now that you have created a network pool, you need to assign this pool to the OvDC.

1. In the system organization, in **Manage and Monitor**, click on **Organization VDCs.**

2. Select the OvDC of your Org and right-click on it.

3. Select **Properties**.

4. In the pop up, select **Network Pool & Services**.

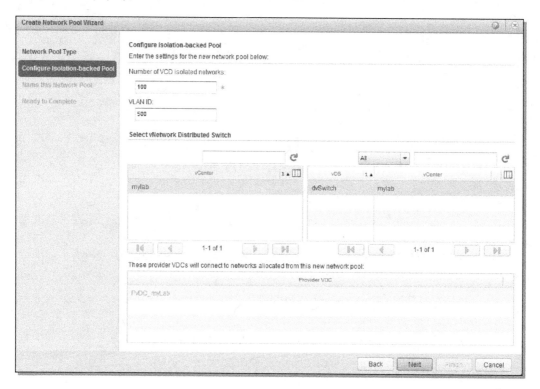

5. Using the drop-down-menu next to **Network pool,** choose the network pool you have just created.

6. Underneath, you will see how many networks are available in this pool. You can now define how many of those should be used in this OvDC.

7. Click on **OK**.

We are now ready to create the vApp and organization networks. Now we need to set the MTU for this pool to 1,600. Make sure that your physical switching infrastructure can use a higher MTU than the default 1,500.

1. Click on the created network pool and select **Properties**.

2. Click on **Network Pool MTU** and set **MTU** to **1600**.

3. Click on **OK**.

> You can create one network isolation-backed network pool and share it with multiple OvDCs in different Orgs just by limiting the numbers of networks you want to use in each.

vApp networks

Now that we have a network pool to draw from, we start our journey into networks by creating a vApp network. We will create a new vApp using our templates and assigning a vApp network to them.

A vApp network is isolated from any other network. This means you can have multiple vApps that use the same network settings without interfering with each other. Each vApp network consists of the following settings:

✦ Gateway address (mandatory)

✦ Network mask (mandatory)

✦ Primary and secondary DNS server

✦ DNS suffix

✦ IP pool

As we already know from the previous segment about templates, a VM inside a vApp will be assigned its network information using guest OS customization. There are three ways for the VM to get its network configuration.

✦ **DHCP**: The VM is configured to receive its information from a DHCP server. The DHCP server either needs to be provided inside the vApp or you can use the DHCP service of vCD.

✦ **Static – IP pool**: An IP address is automatically assigned from the IP pool of the vApp network.

✦ **Static – Manual**: You can enter any IP address that corresponds with the network setting of the vApp network.

We will now create a new vApp with a vApp network.

1. In your organization, go to **My Cloud**.

2. Click on the green + icon to create a new vApp form catalog.

3. Select one of your templates.

4. Give it a name and assign an OvDC and storage profile to it (or just click on **Next**).

5. In the **Configure Network** section we now create our vApp network and tell the VM how to use it.

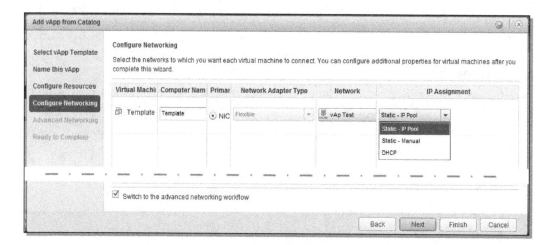

6. Check the checkbox **Switch to the advanced networking workflow**.

7. Then, from the drop-down menu, choose **Add Network....**

8. A new pop up appears, and here, we define the network.

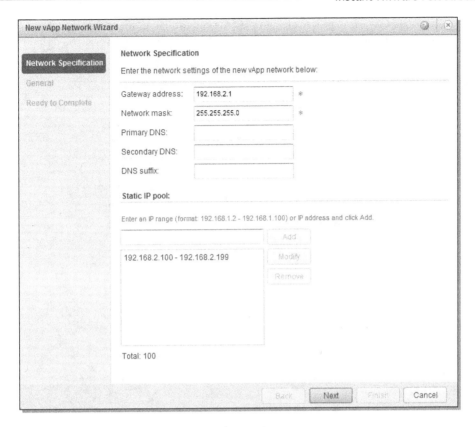

9. vCD has already prepopulated this for easy use. You can either use this information or change it according to your demands.

10. After clicking **Next,** you can define a name for this vApp network.

11. Clicking **OK** will drop us back to the VM assignment. Here, we now assign the way the VM will get its network information from the vApp network. The default is **Static – IP Pool**.

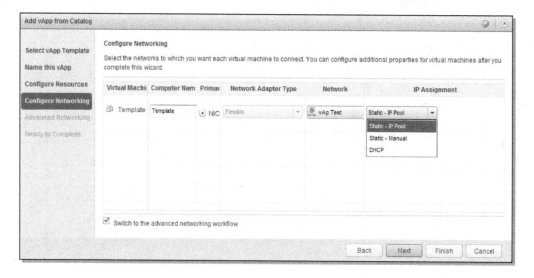

12. Now finish the creation of the vApp and power it on.

13. Check out the VM and its network setting. Check the properties of the vApp and the VM.

We have now created a simple vApp network. I encourage you to:

✦ Investigate the three tabs inside your vApp and see what information they provide you with

✦ Make a template of this new vApp and redeploy it

✦ Look into the other VM network assignments

✦ Have a look at what happens in vCenter when you power on a vApp with a vApp network

✦ Create a VM with multiple network cards and multiple vApp networks (tiered applications)

Organization networks (Org Nets)

Now that you have looked into the basic concepts of vApp networks, let's move on to organizational networks.

There are again three types of Org Nets:

✦ **Isolated**: An isolated Org Net exists only in this organization and is not connected to an external network; however, it can be connected to the vApp networks or VMs.

✦ **Routed (Edge Gateway)**: A routed Org Net allows a connection to an external network using an Edge Gateway. An Edge Gateway allows defining firewall and NAT rules as well as VPN connections and load balance settings. Routed gateways connect external networks to vApp networks and/or VMs.

✦ **Directly connected**: These Org Nets are basically an extraction of an external network into the organization. They directly connect external networks to the vApp networks or VMs.

Creating an Org Net

We will create an isolated Org Net. Routed networks are out of the scope of this book, and directly connected networks will be in the next part of this segment.

1. In your organization, click on **Administration**.

2. Click on **Virtual Datacenters** and then on your OvDC.

3. Click on **Org VDC Networks**.

4. Click on the green + icon to create a new Org Net.

5. In the pop up, select **Create an isolated network....**

6. The next window is similar to the one where we defined the network settings of our vApp network. Fill it in with your settings and click on **Next**.

7. Name your Org Net. Below that you can choose to share this Org Net with all other OvDCs in this organization, which in general is a good idea.

8. Click on **Finish** and check out what is happening in vCenter.

You have now created an isolated organizational network.

Using an Org Net

Now that we have created an Org Net, let's use it. First, we will directly attach VMs to the Org Net, and then, we will attach a vApp network to an Org Net.

1. As before, create a new vApp.

2. In the **Network Configuration** section, you can now see (in the drop-down menu) the Org Net you have created.

3. All the settings are similar to the vApp network setting, including the network setting allocations for VMs.

4. Finish the creation of the vApp and power it on.

5. Check the settings of the VMs and have a look at the vApp details such as the network diagram.

You have now connected VMs directly to an Org Net. This will enable vApps to communicate with each other.

We now connect the Org Net to a vApp network.

1. Create a new vApp with a vApp network.

2. To add the Org Net, go to your vApp and click on the **Networking** tab.

3. Click on the green **+** icon to add a network to the vApp.

4. Now, select **Organization VDC network.**

5. Select the Org Net you would like to add, and finish the wizard.

6. Now you see both the vApp and the Org Net. The Org Net will appear in light yellow to indicate that the settings are not saved yet.

7. Click on the drop-down menu under **Connection** for the vApp network and select **OrgNet**.

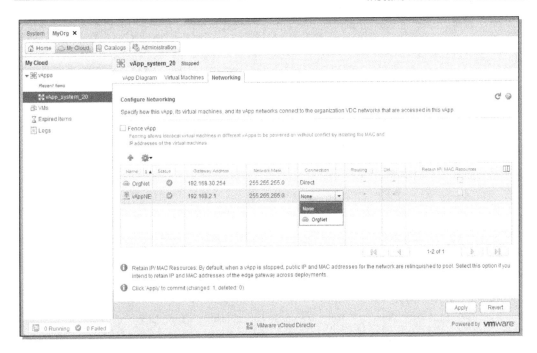

8. vCD automatically adds NAT and firewall services.

9. Click on **Apply** to save the changes.

You have now connected the vApp network to the Org Net and are able to configure NAT and firewall services. To do this, right-click on the vApp network and select **Configure Services**.

External networks

Our last segment here takes us to the external networks. We will create an external network and then connect it to an Org Net.

To create an external network, we need an existing port group that we can use.

1. In the system organization, in **Manage & Monitor**, click on **External Networks**.

2. Click on the green **+ icon** to create a new external network.

3. Select the vCenter and the port group that our external network is connected to.

4. You are now presented with an empty table. Click on **Add** in the lower-left corner.

5. A very familiar pop up appears asking for network information for the external network. The IP pool setting is mandatory as vCD needs IPs to create gateway services.

6. After defining the external network, give it a name and finish the creation.

You have now created an external network. Let's connect the external network to an Org Net.

1. As you did previously, create a new Org Net.

2. This time, select **Connect directly to an external network**.

3. Select the external network you would like to connect to and click on **Next**.

4. Name the organizational network and finish the creation.

You now have an organizational network that is connected directly to an external network. You can now either connect VMs inside a vApp to the external network, via the Org Net, or use NAT and firewall services to introduce some protection between the vApp and the external network.

> You can use firewall and NAT rules to allow, for example, RDP traffic from the external network into the isolated vApp network.

What else is there to explore?

There is quite a lot left to explore. Here are some topics I think would be of interest:

+ Snapshots
+ VXLANs
+ Storage profiles
+ Edge gateways
+ User and group management
+ SSO integration
+ Branding

People and places you should get to know

If you need help with the vCloud, here are some people and places which will prove to be invaluable.

Official Sites

✦ **Homepage**: The main page for all things VMware.

  ◦ `http://vmware.com`

  ◦ `http://vcloud.vmware.com`

✦ **Manual and documentation**: Documentation is a key factor and you should know where to find it. Make sure you read the release notes for each product so you are aware about what has changed, what works, and what doesn't.

  ◦ `http://vcloud.vmware.com/support`

  ◦ `https://www.vmware.com/support/pubs/vmware-vcloud-suite-pubs.html`

  ◦ `http://www.vmware.com/pdf/vsphere5/r51/vsphere-51-configuration-maximums.pdf`

✦ **Knowledge base**: The knowledge base holds articles about bugs and solutions and should be your first point of contact.

  ◦ `http://kb.vmware.com`

✦ **Compatibility guide**: A rather important point of contact is the compatibility guide. It shows you what software and hardware works with what product.

  ◦ `http://www.vmware.com/resources/compatibility/search.php`

✦ **Community**: The VMware-owned communities can provide help and give you a platform to ask questions. It's a good idea to create an account here.

  ◦ `http://communities.vmware.com`

Articles and Tutorials

✦ VMware vCloud Networking and Security 5.1 – evaluation: `http://blogs.vmware.com/vsphere/2012/10/vmware-vcloud-networking-and-security-5-1-evaluation-videos.html`.

✦ vCloud Director and VXLAN: `http://blogs.vmware.com/vcloud/2012/10/vcloud-director-5-1-vxlan-configuration.html`.

  ◦ And with a bit more detail for CISCO users: `http://www.kendrickcoleman.com/index.php/Tech-Blog/how-to-configure-vxlan-in-vcloud-director-step-by-step.html`.

- VCloud Director Edge Gateways (how-to videos)
    - Configure: `http://www.youtube.com/watch?v=e1G1zxGHheg`.
    - Deploy: `http://www.youtube.com/watch?v=v9XOOFhvDBk`.
- vCloud Director and disaster recovery: `http://www.youtube.com/watch?v=I41tS6N0dXY`.

The community

After the VMware communities, the community to belong to is VMUG. VMUG provides an online community, a newsletter, webcasts, and most importantly, organizes local meetings. Also it's free! There is also a paid subscription that gives you a discount on VMware products, online learning courses, and entry fees. Here is the link: `http://www.vmug.com/`.

Blogs

- Duncan Epping's blog; he is quite focused on technical deep drives and has also published several books: `http://www.yellow-bricks.com/`.
- Keeping up with the Jones! A daily overview on vSphere and vCloud whitepapers: `http://searchvmware.techtarget.com/`.
- This one is the same as the previous point but focuses on *all* the cloud and virtualization vendors. It's good to know what everyone else is doing: `http://searchservervirtualization.techtarget.com/`.
- Useful vCD blogs: `http://communities.vmware.com/people/jadelzein/blog/tags/vcd`.
- Check out Tom Stephens's blog. He publishes vCloud Appliance: `http://blogs.vmware.com/vsphere/author/tom_stephens`.

Twitter

- The official VMware vCloud account on Twitter: `https://twitter.com/vcloud`.

About Packt Publishing

Packt, pronounced 'packed', published its first book "*Mastering phpMyAdmin for Effective MySQL Management*" in April 2004 and subsequently continued to specialize in publishing highly focused books on specific technologies and solutions.

Our books and publications share the experiences of your fellow IT professionals in adapting and customizing today's systems, applications, and frameworks. Our solution based books give you the knowledge and power to customize the software and technologies you're using to get the job done. Packt books are more specific and less general than the IT books you have seen in the past. Our unique business model allows us to bring you more focused information, giving you more of what you need to know, and less of what you don't.

Packt is a modern, yet unique publishing company, which focuses on producing quality, cutting-edge books for communities of developers, administrators, and newbies alike. For more information, please visit our website: www.packtpub.com.

Writing for Packt

We welcome all inquiries from people who are interested in authoring. Book proposals should be sent to author@packtpub.com. If your book idea is still at an early stage and you would like to discuss it first before writing a formal book proposal, contact us; one of our commissioning editors will get in touch with you.

We're not just looking for published authors; if you have strong technical skills but no writing experience, our experienced editors can help you develop a writing career, or simply get some additional reward for your expertise.

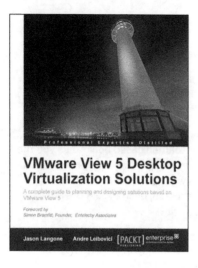

VMware View 5 Desktop Virtualization Solutions

ISBN: 978-1-84968-112-4   Paperback: 308 pages

A complete guide to planning and designing solutions based on VMware View 5

1. Written by VMware experts Jason Langone and Andre Leibovici, this book is a complete guide to planning and designing a solution based on VMware View 5

2. Secure your Visual Desktop Infrastructure (VDI) by having firewalls, antivirus, virtual enclaves, USB redirection and filtering and smart card authentication

3. Analyze the strategies and techniques used to migrate a user population from a physical desktop environment to a virtual desktop solution

VMware ThinApp 4.7 Essentials

ISBN: 978-1-84968-628-0   Paperback: 256 pages

Learn how to quickly and efficiently virtualize your applications with ThinApp 4.7

1. Practical book which provides the essentials of application virtualization with ThinApp 4.7

2. Learn the various methods and best practices of application packaging and deployment

3. Save money and time on your projects with this book by learning how to create portable applications

Please check **www.PacktPub.com** for information on our titles

Citrix XenDesktop 5.6
Cookbook

Implement a fully featured XenDesktop 5.6 architecture in a rich
and powerful VDI experience configuration

Gaspare A. Silvestri

Citrix XenDesktop 5.6 Cookbook

ISBN: 978-1-84968-504-7   Paperback: 354 pages

Implement a fully featured XenDesktop 5.6 architecture in
a rich and powerful VDI experience configuration

1. Real-world methodologies and functioning
    explanations about the XenDesktop 5.6
    architecture and its satellite components used to
    perform a service-oriented architecture

2. Learn how to publish desktops and applications to
    end user devices, optimizing their performance and
    increasing the general security

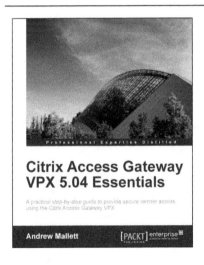

Citrix Access Gateway
VPX 5.04 Essentials

A practical step-by-step guide to provide secure remote access
using the Citrix Access Gateway VPX

Andrew Mallett

Citrix Access Gateway VPX 5.04 Essentials

ISBN: 978-1-84968-822-2   Paperback: 234 pages

A practical step-by-step guide to provide secure remote
access using the Citrix Access Gateway VPX

1. A complete administration companion guiding you
    through the complexity of providing secure remote
    access using the Citrix Access Gateway 5 virtual
    appliance

2. Establish secure access using ICA-Proxy to
    your Citrix XenApp and XenDesktop hosted
    environments

3. Use SmartAccess technology to evaluate end users'
    devices before they connect to your protected
    network

Please check **www.PacktPub.com** for information on our titles

www.ingramcontent.com/pod-product-compliance
Lightning Source LLC
LaVergne TN
LVHW080104070326
832902LV00014B/2409